D0899815

Tracing Books for Kids Ages 3-5
Super Fun Edition

SPEEDY
PUBLISHING

Speedy Publishing LLC
40 E. Main St. #1156
Newark, DE 19711
www.speedypublishing.com

Copyright 2015

All Rights reserved. No part of this book may be reproduced or used in any way or form or by any means whether electronic or mechanical, this means that you cannot record or photocopy any material ideas or tips that are provided in this book

Letters

a a a a a a a

a n n n n n n

a

b b b b b b b

b r r r r r r

b

g g g g g g g

g ʳ ʳ ʳ ʳ ʳ ʳ

g

h h h h h h h

h ʰ ʰ ʰ ʰ ʰ ʰ

h

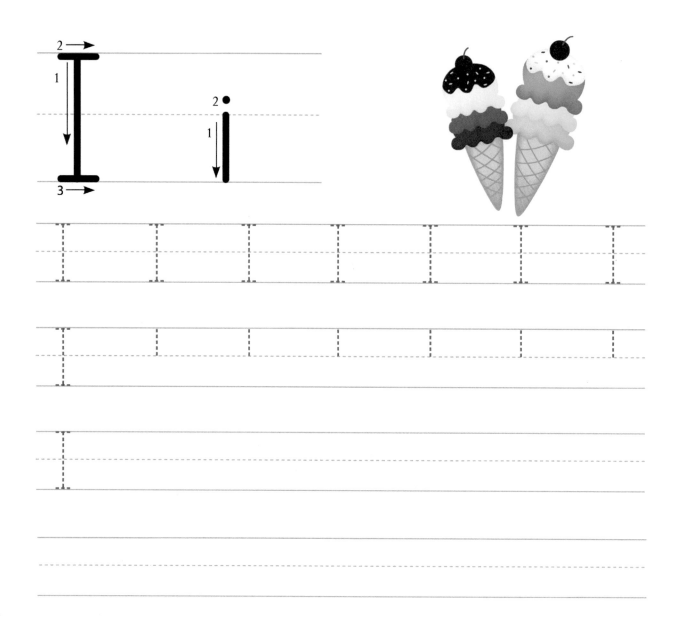

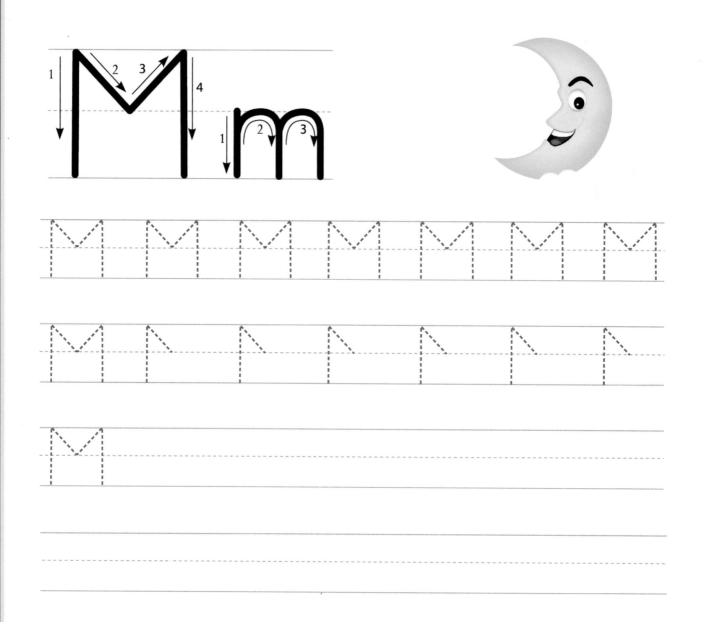

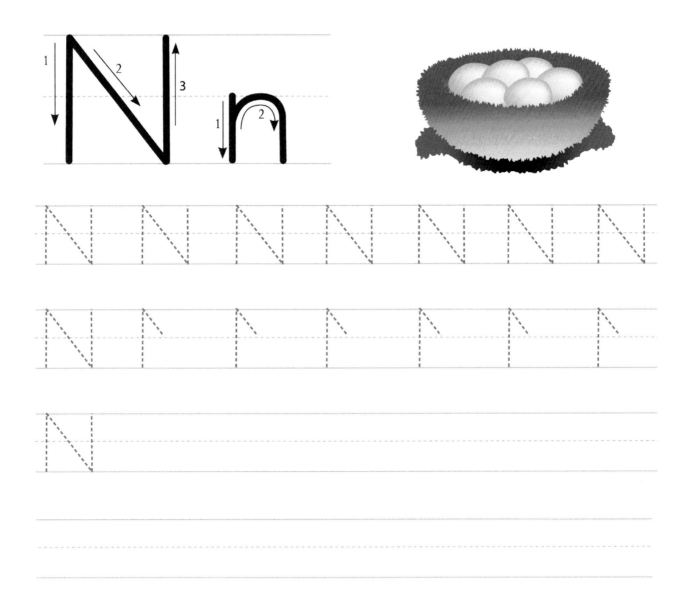

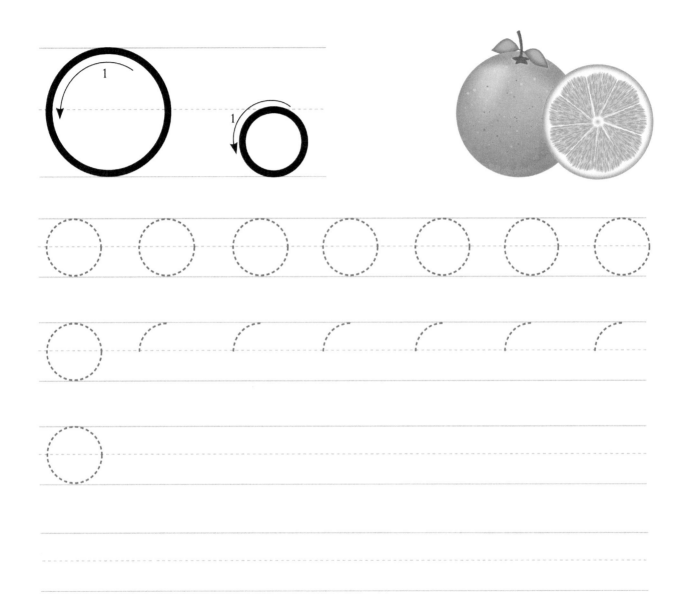

o o o o o o o

o ⌐ ⌐ ⌐ ⌐ ⌐

o

p p p p p p p

p ⌐ ⌐ ⌐ ⌐ ⌐ ⌐

p

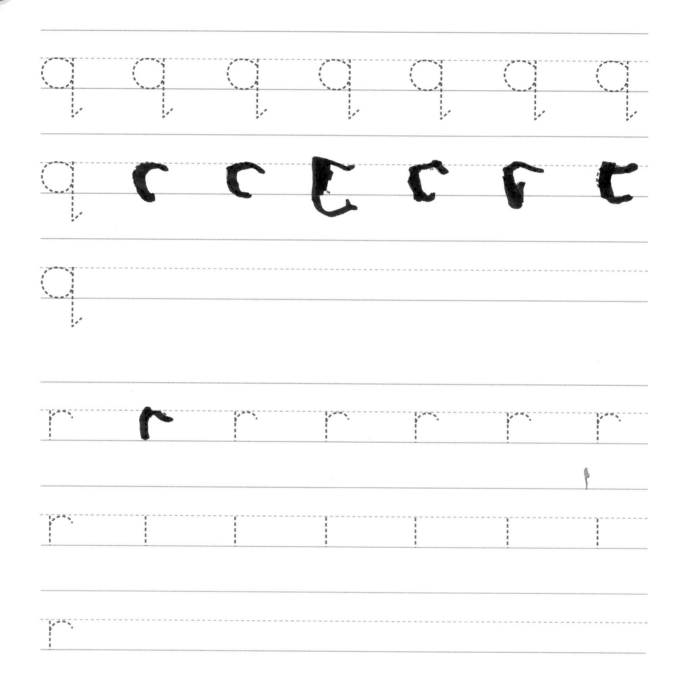

S s

S S S S S S S

s s s s s s s

s

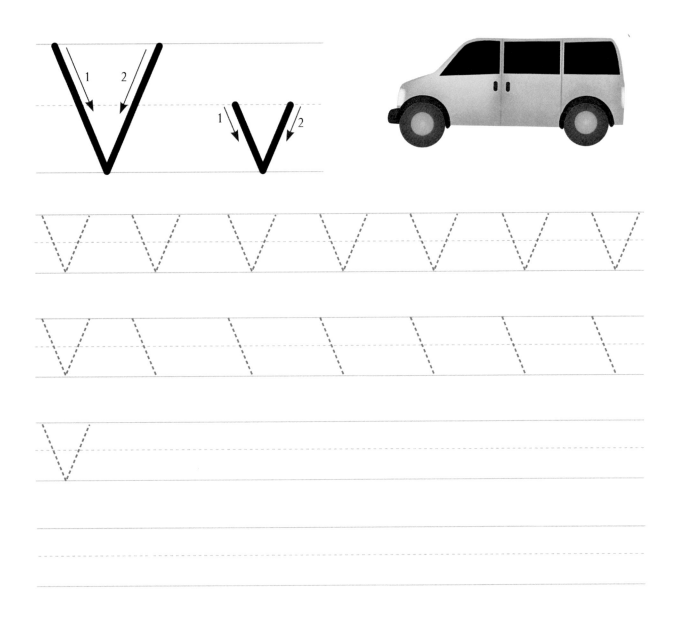

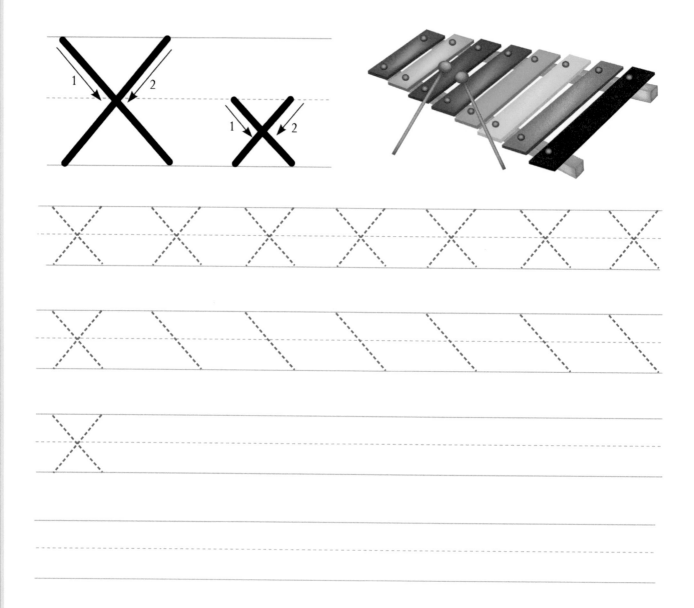

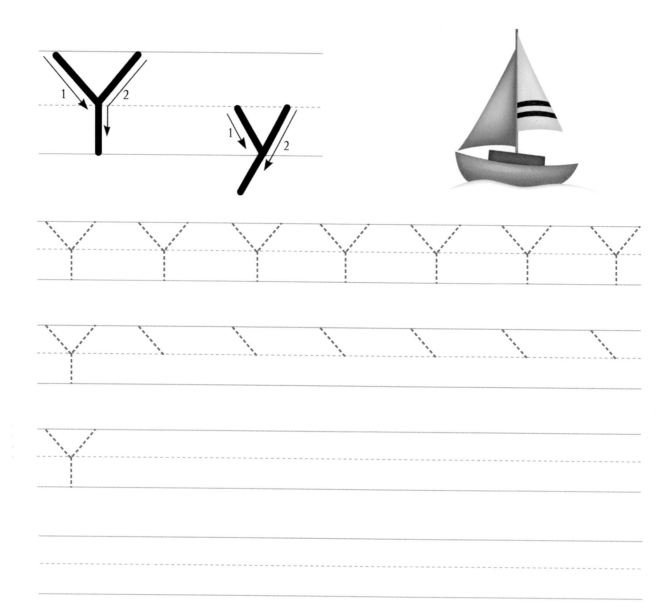

Numbers

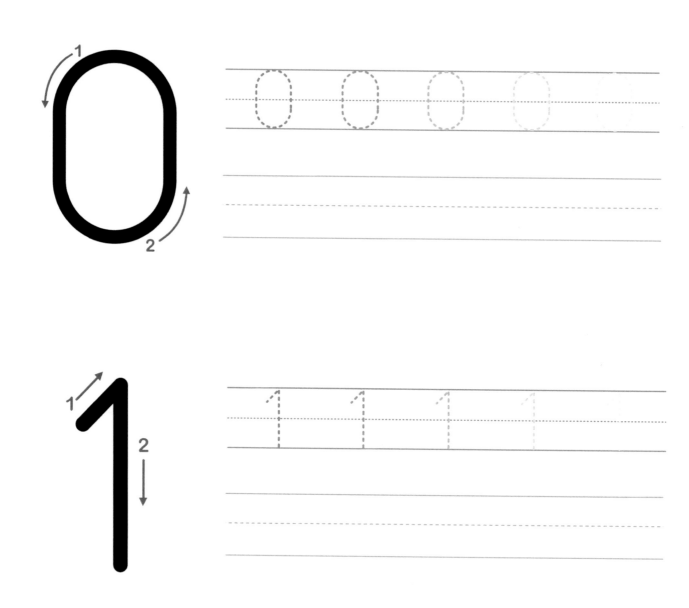

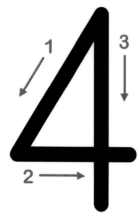

4 4 4 4 4

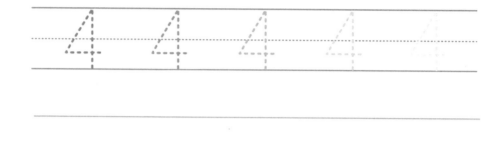

5 5 6 5 5

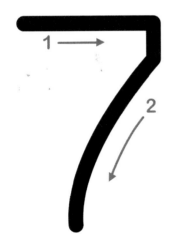

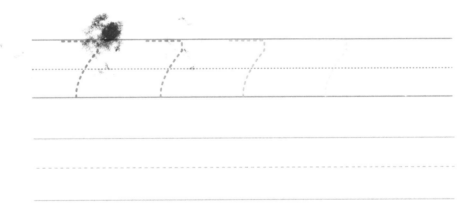

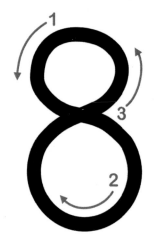

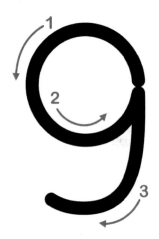